Sydney Z   Dj. Faith

Jessica Gore

Marissa Vernade

AubreyAnna Smith

Jack Finn

Lauren Ridlon

Mike Finn

Greg Wilt

Jordan Diggins

Shravan Sanjiv

Leo

Sharon Hull

Brent Lemeure

Danielle Fenton

Stephanie Culotta

For more information about Alex's Lemonade Stand, please contact
www.alexslemonade.com or orders@alexslemonade.com.

Paje Publishing Company
Text copyright ©2004 by Liz and Jay Scott
Illustrations copyright ©2004 by Pam Howard
Butterfly art on page 31 courtesy of Romero Britto

ISBN 0-9753200-0-9

Printed in the United States

LCCN# 2004092325

This book is the true story of a little girl named Alex. It shows how a small act by one person can grow and have a profound impact on many others. This story is a living example of what the "power of one" can accomplish.

There are many to thank, more than a few,
Patrick, Alex, Eddie, and Joey too.
Our family and friends (both old and new).
To doctors and nurses, the whole hospital crew.
    And, last but not least,
    we applaud those of you
    who know how to make lemonade
    from lemons, too.
    —Liz & Jay

To Carly, Cierra, and Toireasa
    —Alex

To Alex
    —Pam

alex and the amazing lemonade stand

By Liz and Jay Scott

With help from Alex Scott

Illustrations by Pam Howard

This is a story about a **brave** little girl.
She had pretty blue eyes and a head full of curls.

Her name was Alex.

brother

mom

dad

brother

Alex lived with her brothers, her mom and her dad.

She should have been **happy**, but instead she was sad.

Something was wrong, she was not well.

Things were not right, her parents could tell.

The doctor looked her over and said "She is sick.

She needs strong **medicine**. It better be quick."

Alex showed no fear, not even a pout,

Although the medicine made her hair fall out.

"My curls will grow back," little Alex said,

"Now somebody, please, help me out of this bed!"

Alex was determined to feel better again,

but that is not where her determination would end.

Alex was brave and strong and tough

but still the medicine wasn't enough.

She said to herself when she felt sick one day,

"There must be something to make my sickness

go away. What could it be? What can I do

to help myself and others too?"

7

Alex was smart. She developed a plan.
She would sell lemonade from a lemonade stand.

Keeping the money was not in her mind.
She would give it to her hospital
for the cure they might find.

When summer came, Alex told her mother
that she would have her stand with the
help of her brothers.
They **worked** very hard
getting everything ready,
but this work was **fun**, and their
progress was steady.

The day for the sale came round at last.
There were **people** outside;
they were lining up fast!
Many people had heard about Alex's stand,
about little Alex and her lemonade plan.

9

They waited in line, the young & the old,
for a cup of her **lemonade**,
extra sweet and icy cold.

At the end of the day Alex was happy and amazed
to learn how much money her lemonade had raised.
She also learned
something else that was true.
Other people cared about sick kids too.

RECEIVED
AUG 0 6 2003
By

August 5, 2003

Alex,

You are my role model. As a
father of three and a teach
thousands over the l
years, I am
and

I'm very
glad
you got
so much
money.

Your an
all star
A
l
e
x
I knew
you
did it

Lemona
Lane

Dear Alex,
I saw your story in the newspaper and I would like to help you. I make it to... So I am ... you $20 ... lemonade ... you are ... years Old. ...aldron ... I will ... my ...nie

Many people learned of Alex's determination.
They found her story an inspiration.
They sent her cards and wrote her letters.
They liked that she helped sick kids get better.

When **next** year came along,
Alex stuck with her plan.
On another warm Saturday she set up her stand,
people arrived from near and far.
They had heard about **Alex**,
the Lemonade Star.

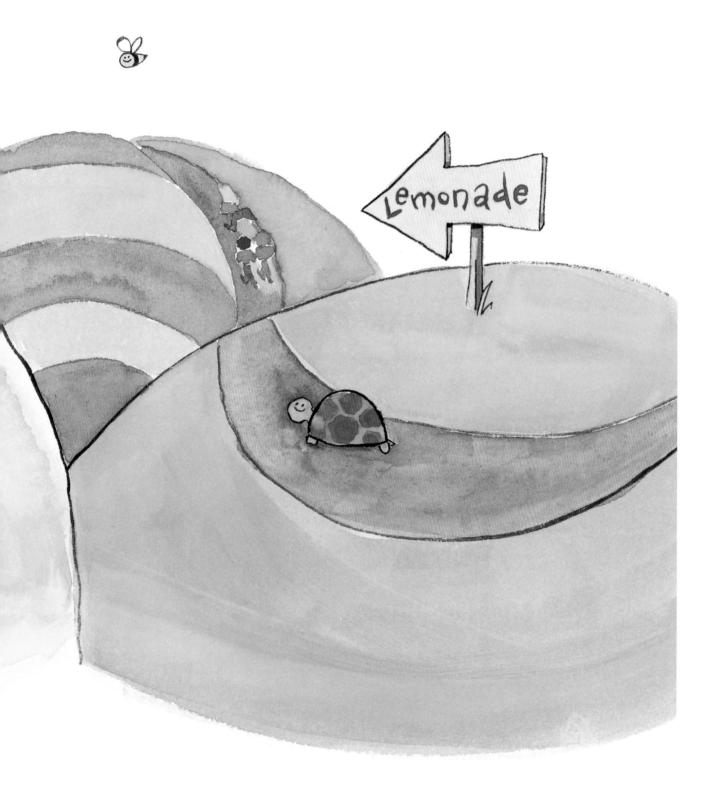

They waited in line, the young & the old,
for a cup of her lemonade,
    extra **sweet** and icy cold.

This year was even better and as her line
grew longer...

...Alex's **determination** for a cure grew stronger.
Again she gave the hospital her money and a letter.

It **said**,

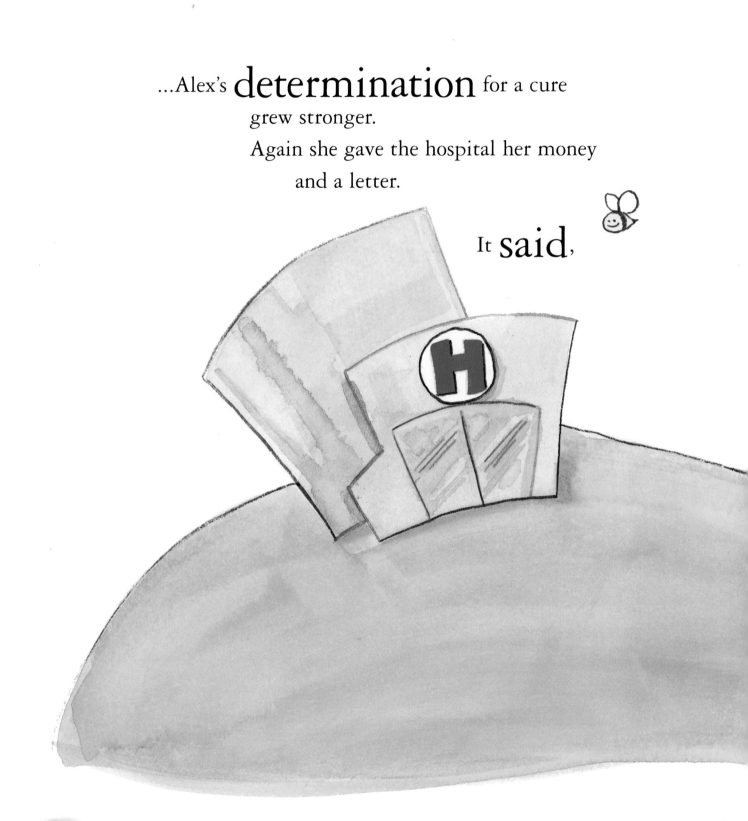

More and more people
heard about the **good
things** that were done
By the girl named Alex
and her Lemonade Fund.

The following year,
Alex had a new plan —

"Now I'll sell lemonade
across this great land!
If more **kids** would help, wouldn't it be great,
we could have lemonade
stands in every **state**.
Think of the money we could raise to
help kids who are sick.
A **cure** might be found,
perhaps even quick!"

Lemonade

Other kids **listened** and held
their own stands,
to help support Alex with her lemonade plans.

21

People waited in line, the young and the old,
they waited for lemonade,
extra sweet and icy cold.

23

These kids sold lemonade and had lots of fun.
Everyone was so **proud** of the good things
they had done.

At the end of the day,
the plan had **succeeded**!
They had raised lots of money
for the **cure**
that was needed.

25

Alex became quite famous,
and caused such a **whirl**,
she came to be known as
"The Little Lemonade Girl"!

Everyone **wondered** how
Alex's story would end.

What could be **next**
for their
lemonade
friend?

She answered that question,

"It's simple, you see,

For this whole thing is not about me.

As long as kids are sick,

I'll do what I can,

to help raise money through

my lemonade stand."

There's a lesson to be learned from

The **Lemonade** Girl

with the pretty blue eyes and

hair that once curled.

You see, Alex lived by the **words**

from which her foundation was laid…

...when **life** gives you lemons,

just make lemonade.

Hold Your Own Stand

Calling all kids across this great land!

You can help kids with your own lemonade stand.

As Alex once said,

"It's easy and it's fun."

You need lemonade, ice, and a little bit of sun.

The money you raise can help kids who are sick.

A cure might be found, perhaps even quick!

Just send it to us, along with a letter,

sending warm wishes that all kids get better.

For more information about how you can help, go to

www.alexslemonade.com

Donations and letters can be sent to:

**Alex's Lemonade Stand
#414
333 East Lancaster Avenue
Wynnewood, PA 19096**

Do you know a young everyday hero who like Alex has done the extraordinary? Consider nominating him or her for the annual **Alex Scott Butterfly Award**—presented by Volvo Cars of North America. The winner receives a contribution from Volvo to the charity of his or her choice. To learn about nominating a young hero, visit **www.volvoforlifeawards.com**.

Alex and the Amazing Lemonade Stand is a true
story about a girl named Alexandra "Alex" Scott and her lemonade stand.
Shortly before her first birthday, Alex was diagnosed with neuroblastoma,
a type of childhood cancer. In the year 2000, when Alex was just four
years old, she told her parents that she wanted to have a lemonade
stand in her front yard. She surprised everyone when she announced her
plan — to donate the money from her stand to "her hospital" to help

the doctors find a cure for all kids with cancer. Even though
Alex continued to bravely battle her own cancer, she also
continued to hold yearly lemonade stands in her front yard
to benefit childhood cancer research. News of Alex, a sick child, helping
other sick children has spread far and wide. People from all over the
world have been inspired by her story and decided to help Alex in her
quest to find a cure. In August of 2004, Alex passed away at the age of 8,
knowing that, with the help of others, she had raised over $1 million to
help find a cure for all kids with cancer. Through Alex's Lemonade Stand,

Alex's family and supporters are enthusiastically carrying
on her efforts to find a cure for childhood cancer, one cup
at a time.

Alex's Lemonade Stand Foundation grew out of Alex's
fundraising efforts and her commitment to finding a cure for childhood
cancers. Alex's efforts have been helped by thousands of caring people
from around the world. These people have helped the cause by making
donations to Alex's Lemonade Stand Foundation or holding lemonade
stands or other fundraisers which support Alex's Lemonade Stand
Foundation for Childhood Cancer.

www.alexslemonade.com